I Have FPIES

A rhyming story of one child's journey with being diagnosed and learning to live with FPIES

Dedicated to my daughter Avery and all the other brave children and families who are living with FPIES.

Copyright: 2023
by Ashlee Ridlon and Avery Ridlon

I was born in October, right before Halloween.
My family loved my hands, toes
and everything in between.

As I grew, I learned how to smile, crawl and coo,
but when I started to eat solid food my Mom said
"There might be something up with you".
I started getting sick, very sick.
My stomach would hurt and I would throw up
so much my family said "ICK!"

I went to the Dr's and I was diagnosed with something you
and I know a lot about. She said I had FPIES and my face made a pout.
We had never heard of this before, but my Dr. said "Have no fear, I will teach you
about it before you head out the door"

We learned about symptoms, the different allergens
and what food trials meant. Some people are
allergic to eggs, milk, rice, oats
or more she said before we went.

My parents would trial me on different foods, like
hamburg, chicken and peas.

My Mom would smile at me after 2 ½ hours
and say the food was safe for me!

But sometimes the food I tried made me sick,
like yogurt and ice cream and eggs benedict.
After a couple hours, I would start to feel bad
and then I would throw up so much my tummy felt sad.

During those times, it could be scary. I didn't like going
to the hospital or getting an iv., it made me wary.
I would sleep a lot after I had my reaction, with my Mom
and Dad by my side. It was hard for them
to see me hurt and to cry.

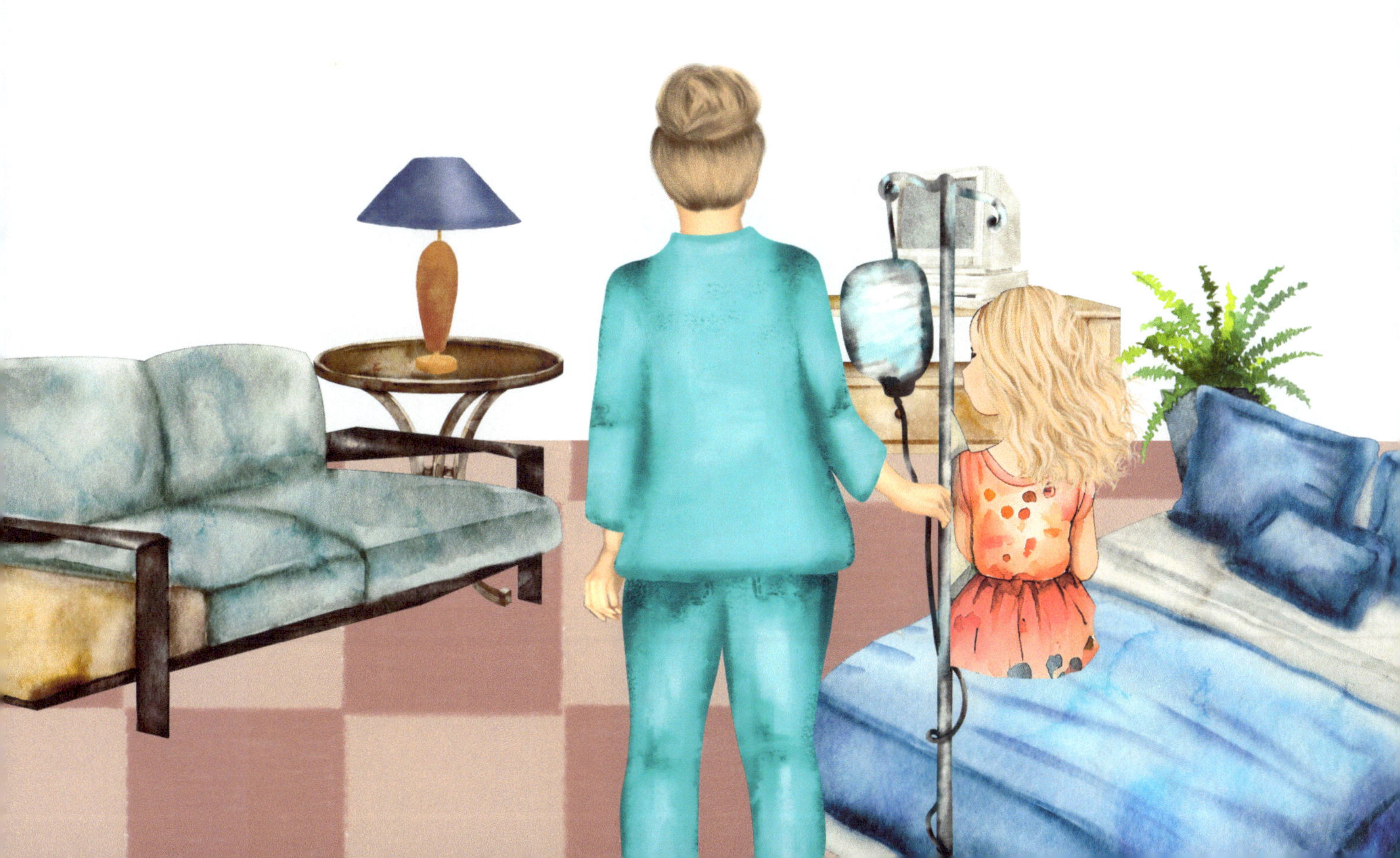

We had good days and bad, just like anyone else. One of the best was when I passed dairy in the hospital, I was beside myself!
After going through the fear of getting an iv. I then had to drink milk and wait with my Mom and Dad to see. And you and I both know that eating something that has made us sick before and could make us sick again, is hard and scary. We have to be brave and it's not always easy! But after 3 hours, I was fine and not sick! I was so excited to get an ice cream and take a big lick!

Other days were harder. Like not passing eggs.
I was already 7, you could tell by my long legs.

I wanted to get McDonalds or eat breakfast
at a restaurant but my body was still allergic and I could not get
what I want.

As the years went by, we learned how to make everything eggless and it was easier than I thought! I learned how to look at ingredients at the store and found food that was safe for me, a lot!

We learned how to live with this new way of eating. We made things like cookies, cakes, pizza and even coconut cheese which stretched just like the real thing; it was misleading!

My Mom and I would bake cupcakes if I was going to a party.
I would teach my friends about FPIES and how it is different for everybody.

They listened closely and learned how eggs would make me sick.
They even learned how to read
ingredients so that they could share food with me quick.

I found some restaurants that were safe for me to eat at.
That was REALLY exciting for me and as I ate my safe chicken tenders,
I would sit and think about that.

Sometimes people don't understand what it's like to
never eat a Happy meal, or not be able to eat the birthday cake
at a party or to try someone's treat and share in the appeal.

So whether you're 2, or 4 or 10, like me,
know that you aren't alone and that I see. I feel
and know and understand what it's like to be you and me.

To have something that is hard and makes us different
is not an easy way to live. But it is who we are and we can learn
and grow and with our words and knowledge, give.

Avery's FPIES Story

Avery was born in October 2012. She was a healthy baby until she began eating solid food around 4 months. She started vomiting to the point of dehydration and shock multiple times, leaving us confused as to what was going on. After many ER visits, an endoscopy and blood tests, we saw an amazing Doctor who recognized the symtoms of FPIES right away. He taught us about her symptoms and what to do moving forward. We immediately stopped feeding her dairy, soy and eggs and started trialing one food each weekend. We started a Safe Foods list on the fridge.

When she reacted to a food, she would vomit severely and get very drowsy. She then would have stomach pain, a fever, and sometimes a fast heartbeat. Her stomach problems lasted several days after the acute episode.

When she was 6, we started to conduct food trials of her trigger foods in the hospital under the watch of doctors. She passed both soy and dairy, which were two of the most exciting days for us all! She trialed eggs three times since and has yet to outgrow it at the present age of 10. Living egg free is not always easy but over the years, we have found many egg free recipes to try and even local restaurants to eat at!
Avery lives with her parents, Ashlee and Nate and brother, Josh in Maine.

Favorite Recipes

Eggless Chocolate Chip Cookies

Ingredients:
- 1/2 cup of butter (one stick)
- 1/4 cup of sugar
- 1/2 cup of packed brown sugar
- 1 1/2 cups of flour
- 1 teaspoon baking soda
- 1 teaspoon of vanilla
- 1 tablespoon of water
- 2 tablespoons of vegetable oil
- 1 cup (or more) of chocolate chips

Pre-heat oven to 350F
Beat butter with sugar until smooth.
Add in water, oil and vanilla and mix.
Add in flour and baking soda to wet ingredients.
Fold in chocolate chips
Use spoon or cookie spoon to drop onto parchment covered baking
sheet and bake for 10 minutes.

Coconut Cheese

A dairy free cheese that stretches like the real thing. It does not have a strong coconut flavor and if eating on pizza with other toppings, it will take on those flavors. Enjoy!

Ingredients

- 1 13.5 oz can coconut milk full fat or coconut cream (13.5 oz can)
- 1/4 cup warm water
- 1 1/4 teaspoons salt
- 2 tablespoons nutritional yeast
- 4 teaspoons agar agar powder
- 1/2 teaspoon garlic powder
- 7 teaspoons tapioca flour (This is the same as 2 tbsp + 1 tsp)
- 1/4 cup cold water

Instructions

- Prepare a glass, ceramic, or silicone mold and have it ready to pour the cheese into when you are done. (I spray mine with a little oil to help it come out easier, but it's not necessary).
- Add a 13.5 oz can of coconut milk (or another cheese base), 1/4 cup of warm water, 1 1/4 tsp salt, 2 tbsp of nutritional yeast, 4 tsp agar agar, 1/2 tsp garlic.
- Heat the cheese sauce over medium heat until it begins to boil.
- Turn down the heat until it is just barely bubbling and allow to boil for 5 minutes while stirring frequently.
- Add 2 tbsp plus 1 tsp (or 7 tsp.) tapioca starch to 1/4 cup of cold water and stir until it dissolves.
- Add the starch and water mixture to the boiling cheese sauce and stir it in with a whisk and cook for an additional 1 minute. (Your cheese will become very thick and stretchy).
- Pour into a glass container and allow to cool uncovered in the refrigerator for at least 3 hours before shredding.
- Store covered in an air-tight container for 5 days in the fridge or up to 3 months in the freezer.

- Credit:https://thehiddenveggies.com/vegan-mozzarella-recipe/

Wacky Cake

INGREDIENTS

For the cake:
1 ½ cups all purpose flour
3 Tablespoons unsweetened cocoa powder
1 cup granulated sugar
1 teaspoon baking soda
½ teaspoon salt
1 teaspoon white vinegar
1 teaspoon vanilla extract
5 Tablespoons vegetable oil
1 cup water

- Preheat oven to 350 degrees F. Spray an 8-inch square pan with nonstick cooking spray.
- Mix first 5 dry ingredients in the prepared pan (flour, cocoa powder, sugar, baking soda and salt.)
- Make 3 depressions in the dry ingredients – two small, one larger.
- Pour vinegar in one of the smaller depressions. Pour the vanilla extract in the other smaller depression and the vegetable oil in third larger depression.
- Pour water over all. Mix well until smooth.
- Bake on middle rack of oven for 35 minutes. Check with toothpick to make sure it comes out clean. Note: Oven baking times may vary, be sure to check your cake to make sure you do not over bake.
- Cool completely before frosting (if using). You can also just sprinkle with a dusting of powdered sugar.

https://sweetlittlebluebird.com/tried-true-tuesday-crazy-cake-no-eggs/

Eggless Brownies

Ingredients:

- 1 1/2 cups of flour
- 1 1/1 cups of sugar
- 1/2 cup of unsweetened cocoa powder
- 1/2 teaspoon baking powder
- 1 teaspoon salt
- 3/4 cup water
- 3/4 canola oil
- 1 teaspoon vanilla extract

Instructions:

- Preheat oven to 350 F. Grease 9"x9" baking pan with oil.
- Sift the flour, sugar, cocoa, baking powder and salt into mixing bowl. Add the water and oil and stir to combine. Stir in vanilla.
- Spread the batter into the prepared pan. Bake for 30-35 minutes or until toothpick inserted in the center comes out clean.
- Cool and enjoy!

Credit: Cookbooks365

About the Author

Ashlee is an author who lives in Southern Maine with her husband and two children. She graduated with a degree in English and then went on to graduate school for elementary education. As a former kindergarten teacher who is still active in her town's elementary school, she loves to combine her love for writing and for children through the writing of children's books.

www.ingramcontent.com/pod-product-compliance
Lightning Source LLC
Chambersburg PA
CBHW042125110726
48006CB00003B/772